Contents

WORSHIP

GROUP STUDIES
LEADER'S GUIDE

Edited by
ANDREW ROBERTS

The Bible Reading Fellowship
15 The Chambers, Vineyard
Abingdon OX14 3FE
brf.org.uk

The Bible Reading Fellowship (BRF) is a Registered Charity (233280)

ISBN 978 0 85746 854 3
First published 2020
10 9 8 7 6 5 4 3 2 1 0
All rights reserved

Text © individual authors 2020
This edition © The Bible Reading Fellowship 2020
Original design by morsebrowndesign.co.uk & penguinboy.net

The authors assert the moral right to be identified as the authors of this work

Acknowledgements
Scripture quotations marked NRSV are taken from The New Revised Standard Version
of the Bible, Anglicised edition, copyright © 1989, 1995 by the Division of Christian
Education of the National Council of the Churches of Christ in the United States of
America. Used by permission. All rights reserved.

Scripture quotations marked NIV are taken from The Holy Bible, New International
Version (Anglicised edition) copyright © 1979, 1984, 2011 by Biblica. Used by
permission of Hodder & Stoughton Publishers, a Hachette UK company. All rights
reserved. 'NIV' is a registered trademark of Biblica. UK trademark number 1448790.

Every effort has been made to trace and contact copyright owners for material used
in this resource. We apologise for any inadvertent omissions or errors, and would
ask those concerned to contact us so that full acknowledgement can be made in
the future.

A catalogue record for this book is available from the British Library

Printed and bound in the UK by Zenith Media NP4 0DQ

About the writers

Liz Hoare is tutor in spiritual formation at Wycliffe Hall in Oxford. She teaches discipleship and prayer and has a special interest in spiritual direction. She is married to Toddy, a sculptor, and they have a son. Liz enjoys baking, the English countryside and looking after her chickens.

Emma Pennington is Canon Missioner of Canterbury Cathedral. Previously, she was vicar of Garsington, Horspath and Cuddesdon and Spirituality Adviser to the diocese of Oxford. She is a regular contributor to the Oxford Diocese and BRF Festival of Prayer and an original member of the organising committee. Emma has a passion for prayer and spirituality and welcomes the opportunity to encourage others to explore the richness of medieval mystical tradition and deepen the contemplative life of prayer. She has given talks and led retreats and Quiet Days both in the UK and abroad, and also tutored and lectured extensively on Christian Spirituality, especially at Oxford University, where she completed her doctoral research on Julian of Norwich in 2014.

Dave Hopwood loves communicating the Bible using contemporary media, language, images and stories. He is author of a fistful of books retelling the Bible including *The Bloke's Bible*, *Diary of a Wimpy Christian* and *Film & Faith*. He passionately believes that the Bible is aimed at ordinary men and women, and that it is earthy, relevant and incisive in the way it tells of God's interaction with the world. These days, he spends much of his time retelling the Bible using anything that seems useful: TV, movies, internet, adverts, news stories, etc. He speaks at various places here, there and everywhere and regularly publishes ideas and material via his website **davehopwood.com**.

Claire Musters is an author, speaker, editor, wife, mother, worship leader and school governor. Her books include *Taking Off the Mask: Daring to be the person God created you to be* (Authentic Media, 2017). You can find out more about her at **clairemusters.com**, where she also blogs on subjects such as discipleship, worship, writing, marriage and parenting, and follow her **@CMusters** and **facebook.com/ClaireMustersWriter**.

Introduction

> They devoted themselves to the apostles' teaching and fellowship, to the breaking of bread and the prayers. Awe came upon everyone, because many wonders and signs were being done by the apostles. All who believed were together and had all things in common; they would sell their possessions and goods and distribute the proceeds to all, as any had need. Day by day, as they spent much time together in the temple, they broke bread at home and ate their food with glad and generous hearts, praising God and having the goodwill of all the people. And day by day the Lord added to their number those who were being saved.
>
> ACTS 2:42–47 (NRSV)

Holy Habits is a way of life to be lived by disciples of Jesus individually and collectively. As Alison Morgan points out in the subtitle of her book *Following Jesus*, the plural of disciple is church. When Jesus calls us to follow, he gifts us others to journey with us, just as he gifted his first disciples – others who will help to teach us and who will learn from us; others who will pray with us and check how we are; others who will watch over us in love and keep us accountable in our discipleship. In the light of this, these Group Studies and the complementary daily Bible Reflections have been written for both group and personal usage. In this booklet, you will find material to help you as a church or a small group reflect together on the particular holy habit being explored.

The authors (who also wrote the complementary Holy Habits Bible Reflections; see page 62) have formed questions for reflection and discussion. Each author has selected two of the readings from the ten they wrote about and provided six questions on each for discussion. Some have a more personal focus, while others relate more to the church or group as whole. With questions of a more personal nature, you may wish to invite people to discuss these in the confidence of pairs and then make time for anyone to share a response with the whole group if they would like to. This approach can also be a good way of making sure everyone has a chance to share if your group has newcomers or people who are shy or dominant.

You will then find a series of take-home questions about the habit. These have been collated from questions submitted by the authors, which mean they vary in style, tone and focus. As such, you may find some more helpful than others, so feel free to add or amend questions. As you work together, you might like to see what emerges in the responses and see if some of the questions should be revisited regularly (perhaps annually or every six months) as a way of reviewing the life of your small group or church as a discipleship community against the picture Luke offers us in Acts 2. Similarly, individuals could be invited to keep a journal to regularly reflect on their living of the holy habits.

In Acts 2:47, Luke says the believers enjoyed 'the goodwill of all the people', so there are also some creative ideas for ways in which your church or group could collectively practise the habit being explored in the local or wider community. These are thought-starter ideas, so be open to other ideas that emerge in your conversations.

You will also find some prayers and creative media ideas for this habit at the back of the book.

In all of this, keep your hearts and minds open to the Holy Spirit and be alert to the wonders of God's grace and the signs of God's love that emerge as, individually and collectively, you live this down-to-earth, holy way of life that Luke invites us to imitate.

Session outline

Session outline

One way your group time could be structured:

- **Opening prayer**
  (for example, the Holy Habits prayer on page 59)

- **Music moment**
  (see 'Listen', page 61)

- **Bible reading**

- **Reflection**

- **Discussion questions**

- **Time for stories, testimonies or questions/issues that arise from the discussion**

- **Prayer**

- **Ideas to do as a group**
  Spend a few minutes to agree when this will be carried out or to come up with other ideas

- **Take-home questions/creative media ideas**

- **Closing prayer**

| Liz Hoare

Week 1

God alone is worthy of worship

Read Exodus 20:2–6

> I am the Lord your God, who brought you out of the land of Egypt, out of the house of slavery; you shall have no other gods before me. You shall not make for yourself an idol, whether in the form of anything that is in heaven above, or that is on the earth beneath, or that is in the water under the earth. You shall not bow down to them or worship them; for I the Lord your God am a jealous God, punishing children for the iniquity of parents, to the third and the fourth generation of those who reject me, but showing steadfast love to the thousandth generation of those who love me and keep my commandments.
>
> (NRSV)

Reflection

Surely no one in the modern western world would talk about bowing down to gods of wood or stone, however exquisitely crafted – would they? The New Testament proclaims as good news that the only way we can know what God is like is through Jesus Christ crucified.

If we don't worship this God, who or what do we worship instead? Just as the ancient Israelites were taught to rehearse the ten commandments and engrave them on their hearts, so we need to keep returning to the Lord Jesus, humble and obedient, lest, consciously or unconsciously, we recreate an image of him that belies his true character.

As God first established his law among his people in Exodus 20, he described himself as a jealous God and one showing steadfast love. How do we reconcile these two qualities? Why did he rescue them from slavery? Simply because he loved them utterly and wanted them for his own. All our ideas of God must stem from this premise, for this God alone is worthy of our wholehearted worship. When other idols creep in – especially our reputation, self-preservation and self-determination – they have to go, but so do our false notions of God.

> The 18th-century hymn by William Cowper asks for 'a closer walk with thee' and if that is our longing we may pray with him: 'The dearest idol I have known, whate'er that idol be, help me to tear it from thy throne and worship only thee.'

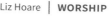
Questions

1 Why do you think the Israelites were constantly being reminded of the exodus? What was its significance for them?

2 What other gods were the Israelites tempted to put in God's place? Why did this problem arise so often in Israel's history?

3 Do you continue to make idols in place of God? How might we do this in church? How does it play out in your personal lives and habits?

4 Do you agree that all our ideas of God are in danger of turning into idols? Can you think of an example of an image of God that you have felt called to let go of? What happened?

5 What does it mean that God is a jealous God? Can you relate your feelings in relation to God's jealousy for his name?

6 How should God's claim to 'punish children for the iniquity of parents' be understood? What light does Jesus' teaching and actions throw on this way of understanding personal and collective responsibility?

● ● ●

Idea to do as a group

1 Choose a passage of scripture that reflects the theme of worship. With your group do some lectio divina, or slow reading, of scripture, meditating on a word or phrase that strikes you and letting it lead you into prayer. (A good introduction to lectio divina is David Foster, *Reading with God*.) How might this become a daily or weekly practice?

Take-home questions

1
What do
think is the
biggest barrier
to honouring
God through
worship?

2
How do
you understand
the relationship
between worship that
encompasses the
whole of life and
what we do in
church?

| Liz Hoare

Week 2

Caring for creation as an act of worship

Read Psalm 8:1–5

O Lord, our Sovereign, how majestic is your name in all the earth! You have set your glory above the heavens. Out of the mouths of babes and infants you have founded a bulwark because of your foes, to silence the enemy and the avenger. When I look at your heavens, the work of your fingers, the moon and the stars that you have established; what are human beings that you are mindful of them, mortals that you care for them? Yet you have made them a little lower than God, and crowned them with glory and honour.   (NRSV)

Reflection

When the writer of this psalm observed the moon and stars in the night sky, it would have been an amazing sight, unhampered by light pollution, stretching across the heavens and constellations forming their patterns, sparkling in the blackness. How small he must have felt! Yet he knew that human beings were the pinnacle of God's creation, created to worship the one who made everything that exists. Even tiny, helpless infants play their part in giving God glory. The only way they can do that is by being themselves, and that includes being vulnerable and needy. Jesus made much of children, stating that we must all become like them in order to enter the kingdom of heaven.

This psalm celebrates creation. Most people say that being outside in creation helps them to pray and to notice signs of transcendence present in the world. We have no excuse today for ignoring the relationship human beings have with the planet. A vital aspect of whole-life worship is the way we treat the created order. We might not think of plastic as an aspect of worship, until, that is, we consider the 'work of God's fingers' and remember that in Genesis he looked at what he had made and saw it was very good. If God is mindful of us, we too must be mindful of one another and work and pray towards a world that enables people to live safely and peaceably. Learning to steward our finite planet for our infinite Lord is our true worship, too.

> Almighty God, creator of heaven and earth, help me to know your loving presence in everything that happens today. Amen

Questions

1 When did you last feel a sense of awe at something in the natural world? What other phenomena fill you with awe and wonder?

2 Do you think it is more difficult to feel small and dependent today than in previous generations? How has the increase in knowledge affected human beings' sense of themselves?

3 Discuss the ways that society thinks of majesty and sovereignty. How are earthly rulers like or unlike God in his sovereignty?

4 What makes you most aware of God's mindfulness concerning humans? In what ways does this manifest itself?

5 Psalm 8 is addressed to God in an attitude of humility. How does the current concern for the future of planet earth move you to worship the God who made it? How could this be a witness to your neighbours?

6 What does it mean that we are made 'a little lower than God?' Is this easy to remember in the way you practise the holy habit of worship?

• • •

Week 2

Idea to do as a group

1 Recognising that the care of creation is an act of
worship, as a group tend a garden, an allotment or
your church grounds as an act of worship in itself.
How might this become a regular worshipful practice
for you as a group?

Take-home **questions**

1

How much does it matter that different Christians worship God with different worship styles (formal vs informal, liturgical vs free-form, silence and symbol vs loud music and exuberant movement)?

2

How might worshipping in different places, indoors and outdoors, deepen and broaden your experiences of God and enrich your worshipping life?

| Emma Pennington

Week 3

Being present

Read Isaiah 1:11–15

'The multitude of your sacrifices – what are they to me?' says the Lord. 'I have more than enough of burnt offerings, of rams and the fat of fattened animals; I have no pleasure in the blood of bulls and lambs and goats. When you come to appear before me, who has asked this of you, this trampling of my courts? Stop bringing meaningless offerings! Your incense is detestable to me. New Moons, Sabbaths and convocations – I cannot bear your worthless assemblies. Your New Moon festivals and your appointed festivals I hate with all my being. They have become a burden to me; I am weary of bearing them. When you spread out your hands in prayer, I hide my eyes from you; even when you offer many prayers, I am not listening. Your hands are full of blood!' (NIV)

Reflection

It's not always easy being the bringer of bad news, but the prophet Isaiah does it with force, clarity and sheer nerve. Writing during a difficult time in the history of the people of God, Isaiah is sent on a daunting task by the Lord. The people have gone astray, rejected the laws of God and broken their covenant with him. Before it gets any worse, Isaiah is commissioned to speak the truth to the people, to show them the error of their ways and hold out the olive branch of forgiveness.

In this passage, we hear the voice of the Lord in the words of Isaiah. They express strong emotions of frustration, annoyance, disgust and despair at the ways in which the people are honouring their Lord in their worship. He does not want their blood sacrifices, offerings, festivals every new moon, feasts and gatherings, practices which have crept into the daily worshipping life of the people from other religions. The faithful observance of the religion of Moses and the law has become corrupt, but, more importantly, outward religious practices have replaced that close and loving relationship between the people and their Lord.

Isaiah's words are specific to a certain age and people, but they are also for us. At the heart of his words is the call to question why we do what we do as people of faith. Saying prayers, going to church, lighting candles, silent times, reading spiritual books – these are all good in so far as they draw us closer to our loving God. But it's easy to get caught up in the doing of worship and forget that at the heart of all we do is the simple desire to just be with the one who loves us and only wants us to be present to him, in all we do say and be. All that we do in the way of spiritual practices is to help, nurture and sustain that relationship in order to honour God, renew ourselves and bless others.

> Be still and know that I am God.

Questions

1   Why is it important to speak out what is right even when it may be costly?

2   Can you think of a time when speaking hard words led to new life?

3   What are your worship practices at this time?

4   Which of these practices do you think you need to lay down?

5   What new ways of worship or being before God do you think God might be calling you to?

6   What helps you become mindfully present to God's love within worship and everyday life?

• • •

Ideas to do as a group

1 Being present to God in yourself – as a group, practise mindfully becoming present to God. Become aware of your body, the feel of what you are touching, the sounds that come to your ears and what you are seeing. Allow your attention to move to your breathing and the gentle rhythm in and out. When thoughts come, let them flow gently through your mind, and if feelings bubble up, acknowledge them but allow them to simply be as you return your attention to your breathing. Simply be who you are in this present and eternal moment – known and loved in God's sight. If it is appropriate, let worship flow from the being.

2 Being present to God in others – challenge each other to mindfully become present to God in other people. Focus your attention on every detail of the other person: their face, clothes, what they say and what is left unsaid. Focus on the other, being non-judgemental, loving and kind. Simply allow the person to be who they are, known and loved by God and see in them the face of Christ. How might you bring that person to mind the next time you worship? You could practise this as a group.

Take-home questions

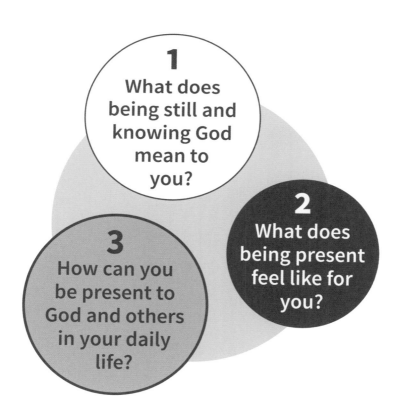

1
What does being still and knowing God mean to you?

2
What does being present feel like for you?

3
How can you be present to God and others in your daily life?

| Emma Pennington

Week 4

The joy of forgiveness

Read Zephaniah 3:14–17

Sing, Daughter Zion; shout aloud, Israel! Be glad and rejoice with all your heart, Daughter Jerusalem! The Lord has taken away your punishment, he has turned back your enemy. The Lord, the King of Israel, is with you; never again will you fear any harm. On that day they will say to Jerusalem, 'Do not fear, Zion; do not let your hands hang limp. The Lord your God is with you, the Mighty Warrior who saves. He will take great delight in you; in his love he will no longer rebuke you, but will rejoice over you with singing.' (NIV)

Reflection

There is something truly wonderful about the moment when, after long time waiting and watching, you see a loved one approaching. With sheer unadulterated joy, a face lights up, recognises you and something truly magical passes between you that no words could ever express. Whether it is between old friends, parents and a child, lover and beloved, it is pure delight in the other's presence. It is this delight, celebration and joy that lies behind the prophet Zephaniah's word. But they come at the end of a long road of reconciliation.

Like the prophets before him and since, Zephaniah has had to speak some hard words to the people of God. Writing at the time of Jeremiah in the seventh century BC, Zephaniah speaks to the people of Jerusalem when they are at an all-time low. Under the previous kings Manasseh and Amon, corruption and immorality has become the norm; now, Zephaniah speaks on behalf of the Lord to a new king, Josiah, and to the people about the coming day of the Lord. In popular parlance, the day of the Lord was associated with a time of unrivalled blessing, when enemies would be toppled and the Lord's reign of justice and peace would prevail. It was a day of hope for the people of God, but for Zephaniah it also a day of reckoning for them. The Lord, who has been long absent in hearts and minds, is coming and few will escape whipping.

Zephaniah's joy here comes at the end of a hard road, one which awakens the people to the reality of their distance with God, calls them to return to faith and seeks forgiveness from the Lord. His song explodes from the freedom which forgiveness brings, when hurts are named, fears are overcome and reconciliation embraced. It is that humbling moment when two people who have fallen out come together once again and renew what had been broken with even deeper cords of love and forgiveness. It is that deep joy which God offers us daily through the cross of Christ.

> Who do you need to forgive?

Questions

1 What would you find hard to forgive?

2 Why is it important to forgive?

3 How does forgiveness differ from reconciliation?

4 Can you think of a time when you felt forgiven?

5 What is the relationship between forgiveness and worship?

6 What gives you joy?

• • •

Ideas to do as a group

1 Praying forgiveness for yourself, as part of your
life of worship – find for yourself a stone. Look
at the stone, focusing on its contours, shape,
colour and texture. Feel the weight of it in your
hand. In Jesus' day, stones were used violently
as weapons of punishment. The gospels tell us
that many wanted to stone Jesus and others
whom they found it difficult to forgive for
the wrongs they had done. As you hold your
stone, reflect on the hard, cold areas of your
life which need the gentleness of forgiveness.
Carefully place the stone down and ask God
to give you the grace to let go and to walk into
the new life which his forgiveness brings to you
through the cross.

2 Praying forgiveness for others, as part of your
life of worship – find the daily news headlines.
Prayerfully read through the stories of the day.
As you do, see in your mind's eye the people
whom they are about. Imagine the backstory
and what is left unsaid, and imagine that you
bring them to the feet of Jesus. In a moment of
silence, pray for God's Spirit of forgiveness to
transform and heal our broken world.

Take-home questions

1
How do you feel about the habit of living a life of worship as one who is forgiven by Christ?

2
Where in your life do you need to ask for the spirit of forgiveness in order to worship with integrity?

3
In what way does this affect how you forgive others?

| Dave Hopwood

Week 5

Offering our gifts

Read Matthew 2:9–12

> After [the Magi] had heard the king, they went on their way, and the star they had seen when it rose went ahead of them until it stopped over the place where the child was. When they saw the star, they were overjoyed. On coming to the house, they saw the child with his mother Mary, and they bowed down and worshipped him. Then they opened their treasures and presented him with gifts of gold, frankincense and myrrh. And having been warned in a dream not to go back to Herod, they returned to their country by another route.
>
> (NIV)

Reflection

These wise men worked hard to find the new king, at first going to the deeply insecure Herod. But the wise men didn't give up; they continued until they were led to Bethlehem, and to this tiny, accessible king, humble and vulnerable, born to courageous parents. On finding Jesus, the travellers brought gifts which were particular to them and offered these as their act of worship.

This Epiphany story is a great reminder of the ways of God. He chooses humble, regular folk in Mary and Joseph, and there is a cost for them in following God's call. Then these wise men turn up from another culture – two sets of very different people brought together by the compassion of God. And in their obedience and travelling, both groups worship Jesus: Mary and Joseph with their time, energy and faithful parenting; the wise men with their three precious gifts.

We are invited to follow in their footsteps: to worship with our time and energy, and with the particular and varied gifts we have been given. In my work as a writer and speaker, I offer my writing to God as my worship, and when I speak I use my passion for contemporary culture as a vehicle for passing on God's love.

What gifts do you have that you could offer to God for his use? What draws your focus and energy? Why not offer these today as worship, and as vehicles for passing on God's love?

> Lord, my strengths and gifts don't always feel very spiritual. but I offer who I am to you. Please help me to use my talents and abilities for you today. Amen

Questions

1 What do you enjoy doing in life? What do you get passionate about?

2 What gifts do you recognise in others in your group? You could pass around sheets of paper with each person's name on it and write down encouraging comments.

3 Can you help others in your group to recognise the godliness of their strengths, gifts and passions? Suggest ways they might use them for God this week as acts of worship (especially if their gifts don't appear to be 'spiritual' to them).

4 What things stop you sharing your gifts with others or make it difficult to do so?

5 Are you aware of situations when you or others have used your gifts, and only later discovered these were unexpectedly helpful or significant?

6 Could you pray for each other now and each day this week, for specific opportunities for sharing your gifts, strengths and passions in ways that honour God?

• • •

Idea to do as a group

1 Get some small business cards printed which say something like, 'Well done. Really like what you did there.' This shouldn't be too expensive, and you could share the cost among those in the group who can afford it.

Share the cards among the group and, when you see someone doing something helpful or kind this week, hand them a card to encourage them. Pray that God will provide opportunities to hand out one or two cards. How might their smile on receiving the card be a reflection of worship? This may start a conversation too.

Take-home questions

1

What do you think about this notion of worship as expressed in the things you do in your day-to-day life? Is this a new idea for you?

2

In the film *Chariots of Fire*, Christian athlete Eric Liddell says, 'God made me fast, and when I run I feel his pleasure.' Do you ever get a sense of that when you use your strengths and abilities to honour God in your daily living?

| Dave Hopwood

Week 6

Extravagant dedication

Read Matthew 26:6–11

While Jesus was in Bethany in the home of Simon the Leper, a woman came to him with an alabaster jar of very expensive perfume, which she poured on his head as he was reclining at the table. When the disciples saw this, they were indignant. 'Why this waste?' they asked. 'This perfume could have been sold at a high price and the money given to the poor.' Aware of this, Jesus said to them, 'Why are you bothering this woman? She has done a beautiful thing to me. The poor you will always have with you, but you will not always have me.'

(NIV)

Reflection

At a million pounds a bottle, DKNY produce the most expensive perfume in the world. This jar is not quite in that league, but it was worth a lot of money. Pouring it over Jesus would have filled the house with a beautiful aroma, one that may well have lingered as a reminder of Jesus's life and compassion. This woman offered her extravagant act of worship, and, rather than being called wasteful, Jesus predicted that she would go down in history for doing it.

A friend once took me to Cambodia. I was struck by his generosity – in paying for my trip, doing all he could to serve the people we met and then, back here in the UK, sharing his life with friends and family. His extravagance impressed me. Wherever he was, among rich or poor, he was generous. Perhaps this woman's generosity impacted Peter, Mary, and the other disciples. They would surely never forget her actions and Jesus's response.

Generous worship costs. It might well draw upon our money, time, priorities or energy. But it can be powerful, and it sometimes speaks volumes. It cost this woman dearly – but for her, worshipping Jesus in this way was worth it. It's not easy, but it can be a vital expression of our dedication to God.

Reflecting on the generosity of others, can you recall a time when someone was extravagant towards you? How did you feel? How might that influence how you worship?

> Thank you, Lord, for the kindness of those who have helped me in the past. May my worship be fragranced with kindness and generosity. Amen

Questions

1 Jesus lived generously, sharing what he had of his time, energy and talents. Can you think of examples of this from the gospel accounts?

2 How many different ways can a person live generously? Try making a list together as a group. How might these be expression of worship?

3 What most holds you back from being generous? For example, you may want to discuss peer pressure, busyness, fear of being laughed at, past experiences.

4 Do you ever feel like the disciples in this passage, having a good reason to hold back?

5 How generous is your group or church as a whole when it comes to worship? (For example, how much of your church budget is allocated to worship?)

6 Do you pray for opportunities to live generously as part of a worshipful lifestyle? Can you do that together now as a group?

• • •

Week 6

Idea to do as a group

> **1** As an act of worship, offer to help any people you know who might need shopping done or other practical assistance. Even just chatting with them can be helpful. If you can fix cars, put up shelves, cut lawns, bake cakes, write letters and so on, you might be able to offer help with other things too.

Take-home question

1

In Exodus 31:1–6, we read that God has given Bezalel, Oholiab and others some very practical spiritual gifts. What do you think about this? Does the nature of their gifting surprise you? Do you have any of these gifts? How might these be ways in which you can express your worship?

| Claire Musters

Week 7

Living sacrifices

Read Romans 12:1–2

> Therefore, I urge you, brothers and sisters, in view of God's mercy, to offer your bodies as a living sacrifice, holy and pleasing to God – this is your true and proper worship. Do not conform to the pattern of this world, but be transformed by the renewing of your mind. Then you will be able to test and approve what God's will is – his good, pleasing and perfect will. (NIV)

Reflection

Whenever a passage starts with the word 'Therefore', I am always keen to find out what came before it. In Romans 11, Paul finishes with what is often referred to as a doxology. It can be summed up in the final verse: 'For from him and through him and for him are all things. To him be the glory forever! Amen' (v. 36). Whenever we take time to really consider God's greatness, and, as our passage reminds us, his mercy, the appropriate response is worship.

But what does that mean for us in our everyday lives? Paul is urging us to offer ourselves up wholly as a 'living sacrifice' to God. In the Old Testament, God's people had to offer up animal sacrifices in order to draw near to him. Jesus' ultimate sacrifice on the cross made those no longer necessary, but 'true and proper worship' still demands a sacrifice from us. It is about putting aside our own wants and desires, and taking the time to find out what God's will is – and what it means to be holy before him.

The second half of our passage is a very practical reminder for our daily lives. We are constantly bombarded by messages through social media, advertising, etc. that we can take on board without realising. Here we are told to 'be transformed by the renewing of your mind'. We need to actively consider what we allow into our minds. Rather than simply just accepting whatever thought flits in, whatever material we see in front of us, we have a choice. We can also feed ourselves regularly on the most beneficial material of all: the Bible.

> Lord, help me today to offer up my whole self to you, including my mind. I want my worship to include living out your will well each day. Amen

Questions

1 Why do you think Paul is so urgent in his
message here?

2 Explore together different ways in which you can
offer your bodies as living sacrifices.

3 In what ways do you think we conform to the
'pattern of this world', and how does this dull
our worship?

4 Discuss honestly together what TV programmes
you are watching, what magazines and websites
you are reading and what conversations you
have allowed yourself to be a part of. Is all this
edifying? Positive? Helpful?

5 Think about how much you are feeding on the
word of God. Do you need to increase your
input? Be honest with one another and decide to
hold each other accountable as you do this.

6 How is discovering and living out God's will an
act of worship?

• • •

Idea to do as a group

> **1** Explore ways that you can worship creatively as a
> community of believers (for example, put on some
> worship music, have a giant sheet of paper with
> paint and each paint a response). Choose one idea
> to engage with each week for the next month.

Take-home questions

1

How do you respond to the idea that worship is often about daily sacrifice and discipline?

2

'Holy and pleasing to God – this is your true and proper worship.' In a private space reflect on these words. How does the worship you offer day by day seem in the light of these words? What extra grace may you need at this time?

| Claire Musters

Week 8

Living wisely

Read Ephesians 5:15–20

> Be very careful, then, how you live – not as unwise but as wise, making the most of every opportunity, because the days are evil. Therefore do not be foolish, but understand what the Lord's will is. Do not get drunk on wine, which leads to debauchery. Instead, be filled with the Spirit, speaking to one another with psalms, hymns, and songs from the Spirit. Sing and make music from your heart to the Lord, always giving thanks to God the Father for everything, in the name of our Lord Jesus Christ.
>
> (NIV)

Reflection

It is far too easy to be apathetic – or over-busy and tired. As a result, we end up living just like everyone else, with God tagged on to the rest of our lives, rather than living wisely. We need to realise when we are doing this and be proactive. We have already seen in the passage in Romans 12 that we can understand God's will more fully when we are transformed by the renewing of our minds. Filling our hearts and minds with the word of God is a vital act of worship. So, too, is being filled with the Spirit. The verb here is actually the present continuous in the original – so a more accurate translation would be 'go on being filled'. We can, and should, ask for the empowering of the Holy Spirit every day.

The importance of sung worship is emphasised in today's passage too, both corporate and individual. We are told to speak and sing to one another – this is something my shyness and 'British-ness' made difficult, but I have experienced the encouragement of a friend singing a psalm over me. I also attended a singing workshop once, where were told to get into small groups of people (that we didn't know) and to sing over each other. It took a big step of faith – and courage – but was so powerful.

Individually, heartfelt worship can flow up out of a deep sense of gratitude, so this is a great reminder to choose to be thankful every day.

> Lord, I am so grateful for this new day, and for the breath of life you have placed in me. Help me to live wisely, through the power of your Holy Spirit.

Questions

1 What are some ways you can live unwisely?

2 Look back over the past few days, asking God to open your spiritual eyes to see the ways he provided for you to share his love with others. In what ways were these acts of worship?

3 Share together what experiences you have of being filled with the Spirit. You might like to pray for a fresh infilling after you have shared.

4 Have you ever spent some time singing over one another, perhaps using a psalm or a word you feel is from God? Be brave and try doing so now.

5 Share ways in which you 'sing and make music from your heart' during the week. You may give each other new ideas to try.

6 Why is gratitude so helpful?

● ● ●

Ideas to do as a group

1 God has compassion for the poor and oppressed. Is your church involved in ministries for the poor? If so, get involved in helping out in some way. If not, find a local charity that is and offer your services, as you are able to. Take time to reflect on how serving in these ways is worshipful.

2 As a group, agree to do the gratitude challenge: write down five things you can be thankful for God each day for a week and then report back. (You might like to start by each sharing one point of gratitude while you are together.)

Take-home questions

1
Do you think that the western church worships the majestic, holy, awesome Lamb or is the emphasis on him being our friend? How can you ensure you get the balance right in your own life?

2
Why is worshipping together corporately so important?

For your notes

For your notes

Prayers

The Holy Habits prayer

Endurance produces character, and character produces hope,
    and hope does not disappoint us…
Gracious and ever-loving God, we offer our lives to you.
Help us always to be open to your Spirit in our thoughts
    and feelings and actions.
Support us as we seek to learn more about those habits of
    the Christian life
which, as we practise them, will form in us the character
    of Jesus
by establishing us in the way of faith, hope and love.
Amen

A responsive prayer of praise

When life is good and my heart feels glad
I will praise you, beautiful God

When life is dull and every day feels the same
I will praise you, beautiful God

When I feel hopeful and life is falling into place perfectly
I will praise you, beautiful God

When I feel no hope for the future and I can't see a way forward
I will praise you, beautiful God

When life is wonderful and those I love are thriving
I will praise you, beautiful God

When I get wrapped up in myself and my own concerns
I will praise you, beautiful God

Prayers

When I get overwhelmed with the world and all the need
I will praise you, beautiful God

Because I am your friend and disciple, because I know
your heart
I will praise you, beautiful God

Whatever the circumstance, because of who you are
I will praise you, beautiful God
I will praise you, beautiful God

A prayer to the holy God

Holy God, we know that, however difficult it may be at times,
worshipping you draws us in,
helps to mould us to the person that you want us to be,
helps us to bring your love into a broken world.
Help us to use all our senses in worshipping you.
Holy God, lead us into worship with you.
Amen

Creative media ideas

Watch

Sister Act (PG, 1992, 1h40m)

When a nightclub singer who has witnessed a horrific gang crime is disguised by the police as a nun in a traditional convent, neither the convent nor the singer will ever be the same.

- What does this film have to teach us about stepping outside our 'comfort zones'?
- What might we learn about the exuberance and sincerity of worship?

Read

The Worship-Driven Life: The reason we were created by A.W. Tozer (Monarch Books, 2008)

The supreme importance of worship: the purpose of humankind and the expectation of God.

Listen

'Praise You in This Storm' by Casting Crowns

Whole-church resources

Individual copy £4.99

Holy Habits is an adventure in Christian discipleship. Inspired by Luke's model of church found in Acts 2:42–47, it identifies ten habits and encourages the development of a way of life formed by them. These resources are designed to help churches explore the habits creatively in a range of contexts and live them out in whole-life, intergenerational, missional discipleship.

MISSIONAL DISCIPLESHIP RESOURCES FOR CHURCHES

HOLYHABITS

Original design by morsebrowndesign.co.uk & penguinboy.net

These new additions to the Holy Habits resources have been developed to help churches and individuals explore the Holy Habits through prayerful engagement with the Bible and live them out in whole-life, missional discipleship.

Bible Reflections   Edited by Andrew Roberts | Individual copy £3.99

Each set of Bible reading notes contains eight weeks of devotional material. Four writers bring different perspectives on the habit in question through their reflections on passages drawn from across the Bible narrative.

Group Studies   Edited by Andrew Roberts | Individual copy £6.99

Each leader's guide contains eight sessions of Bible study material, providing off-the-peg material to help churches get started or continue with Holy Habits. Each session includes a Bible passage, reflections, group questions, community/outreach ideas, art and media links and a prayer.

Find out more at holyhabits.org.uk
and brfonline.org.uk/collections/holy-habits
Download a leaflet for your church leadership at
brfonline.org.uk/holyhabitsdownload

Praise for the original Holy Habits resources

'Here are some varied and rich resources to help further deepen our discipleship of Christ, encouraging and enabling us to adopt the life-transforming habits that make for following Jesus.'

Revd Dr Martyn Atkins, Team Leader & Superintendent Minister, Methodist Central Hall, Westminster

'The Holy Habits resources will help you, your church, your fellowship group, to engage in a journey of discovery about what it really means to be a disciple today. I know you will be encouraged, challenged and inspired as you read and work your way through… There is lots to study together and pray about, and that can only be good as our churches today seek to bring about the kingdom of God.'

Revd Loraine Mellor, President of the Methodist Conference 2017/18

'The Holy Habits resources help weave the spiritual through everyday life. They're a great tool that just get better with use. They help us grow in our desire to follow Jesus as their concern is formation not simply information.'

Olive Fleming Drane and John Drane

'The Holy Habits resources are an insightful and comprehensive manual for living in the way of Jesus in the 21st century: an imaginative, faithful and practical gift for the church that will sustain and invigorate our life and mission in a demanding world. The Holy Habits resources are potentially transformational for a church.'

Revd Ian Adams, Mission Spirituality Adviser for Church Mission Society

'To understand the disciplines of the Christian life without practising them habitually is like owning a fine collection of soap but never having a wash. The team behind Holy Habits knows this, which is why they have produced these excellent and practical resources. Use them, and by God's grace you will grow in holiness.'

Paul Bayes, Bishop of Liverpool